A PRACTICAL GUIDE FOR
RECRUITMENT
& RETENTION

The most complete manual on recruiting and retention for beginning instrumental music, compiled from ideas and practices of music teachers, music dealers and the music products industry.

Part 1 – Recruitment

Part 2 – Retention

Foreword

Recruiting for beginning instrumental music is a year-round job. Although the director's task may be challenging, there is a great deal and variety of help available.

This booklet describes recruiting methods being used successfully today by directors in schools throughout the country. Some methods differ widely, but all are techniques that have been tested in action and are proven to work. The content here reflects the combined experience of successful educators and school music dealers. That is why this is a practical guide to recruiting and retention for veteran teachers, beginning teachers and future teachers.

One key person not in this booklet is you. It is up to you to add your personality and style to the techniques explained. You can do this by:

- Rewriting the sample letters
- Designing your own forms
- Setting up schedules that fit your school system
- Giving everything your personal touch

The yearly cycle presented in this publication is designed to increase the number of students recruited and keep them in the program. Two methods to improve retention run through this booklet:

- Don't miss any prospective students, especially the good ones – high quality is one of the keys to retention
- Don't try to avoid dropouts – rather, strive to improve retention

This entire booklet is contained on the MAC Flash Drive. You can tailor any of the template examples to your need. This booklet is also available as a downloadable pdf on our website at www.musicachievementcouncil.org.

PART 1 - RECRUITMENT

This guide will explain how successful teachers and music dealers have made the recruitment process an exciting and vital part of the overall program.

Introduction

If it were necessary to explain or justify the study of music to you, you would not be reading this guide. Children don't need justification — they just want to play because it looks like fun. Fortunately, music education has been the subject of countless scientific studies showing its value to children as part of their total education. Without a well-planned and organized recruiting effort, however, most public school instrumental music programs would not thrive.

For a number of reasons, recruiting enough students to keep instrumental music healthy is becoming more important and more difficult at the same time:

- In many areas, school enrollment is declining
- There are more demands on students' time and academic schedules
- There are more homes with two working parents and single parents
- School budgets are being cut
- There continues to be an emphasis placed on academic and high-stakes testing

Two details can make this situation exceptionally challenging
- There isn't much you can do about many of these issues, but that's OK.
- Many administrations and school boards base budget decisions on student numbers—this is OK too, but to ensure healthy enrollment, it is vital to the future of instrumental music to recruit and retain as many students as possible.

Children join an instrumental music program (band, orchestra, guitar or mariachi) and stick with it if:
- The director is enthusiastic and makes learning fun
- Parents, community and school boards support the program
- The instrumental music program is visible in the community

So this is what you have to do:
- Foster student interest
- Communicate regularly with parents
- Develop an ongoing program for nurturing the support of the school's students and staff, the administration and the community

Organize for Success

Recruiting for instrumental music is still full of mysteries and surprises. To help you in this process, there are three very important people you should know.

- The school secretary, who will help set up the recruiting program and open lines of communication within the school and with your students and their parents
- The head custodian, who is the key to assisting in the organization of the in-school facilities
- The full-service music dealer, who will handle your rentals, repairs, music and accessories, and whose representative will visit you on a regular basis

Quick Checklist for Choosing a Music Dealer

Do they provide the following?
- Regular visits by an educational representative — often a former music educator
- Sales and service departments that are readily accessible by phone, fax and e-mail
- A large inventory of music, advocacy support, and educational materials, including an approval plan
- A complete repair service, including loaner instruments
- An extensive line of accessories for all instruments
- An order, delivery and collection system that will not make demands on your time
- A choice among the most widely accepted instrument brands
- Materials for making your entire program run more smoothly — including music folders, administrative forms, schedule calendars, audio/visual aids and materials available from the music products industry
- Studio facilities and private teachers who may also be important assets to your program

Orchestrate Your Publicity

Although newspapers, television and e-mail are the fastest and most effective means of reaching a large number of people to publicize concerts and various events, they may not be the most effective way of successfully reaching students and parents as part of your recruitment program. Your entire music education department must continually advocate the value of a complete music education. In addition, you must emphasize to the parents of potential students the value of participating in instrumental music.

Empower current students to become actively involved in the development of PR materials such as ads, fliers, videos, and social media strategies that can be used in any of the outlets below.
- Your school district's website to promote the program to the entire community
- Your individual school's website to promote the program to the parents of all of the students enrolled at your school
- Your own music department website
- Social media
- School assemblies
- School bulletin boards—both at your school as well as at your feeder schools
- School newspapers
- School announcements

- School and district newsletters—create a quarter-page Music Corner in the school's newsletter and fill with relevant information on a regular basis
- PTA announcements and communiques
- Direct communication by phone, fax and e-mail
- Concert programs
- School faculty—be sure to enlist their help in identifying promising students

Enlist Dealer Help

Educational representatives are experienced in working with music educators in organizing successful recruiting programs. Most have extensive experience and can help in setting-up and carrying out demonstrations as well as testing and implementing follow-up techniques to keep students in the program.

Understand the School Calendar

There are many in-school and after-school activities, so enlist the aid and support of school staff, especially the principal. You will need to set dates and times well in advance to avoid conflicts so the following are as successful as possible:

- Instrument demonstrations at feeder schools as well as within the home school
- Student surveys
- Parent meetings
- First Performance Demonstration Concert
- Mass Band/Orchestra/Guitar/Mariachi Concert
- Petting Zoos

Recruitment Preparation

- Meet with classroom teachers and general music teachers to help plan the recruiting process and identify potential future instrumentalists
- Gather information pertaining to the scholastic level, natural ability, work habits and level of self-discipline of prospective students.

Select and Collect Recruiting Materials

Get to know what materials are available from the music products industry and work with your music dealer to choose the materials that will work best for you.
Materials available may include:

- DVDs
- Posters
- Surveys and survey forms
- Pamphlets for parents and students
- Research-based brochures

Make your requests well in advance and be sure your dealer or supplier knows:

- What you want
- How many you want
- When you need the materials

Recruiting Is a Year-Round Job

Recruiting and retention to-do list:

- Communicate! Communicate! Communicate! Always talk up your wonderful program!
- Inform students and parents
- Inform others including administrators, teachers, PTA, press and other appropriate media outlets
- Meet with students and parents
- Cultivate interest
- Survey students
- Have students choose instruments
- Equip students through rental or other programs
- Sustain student interest
- Engage parent support
- Always provide satisfying and rewarding musical experiences
- To enhance the performance experience for your beginners, schedule the *First Performance Demonstration Concert*, which is available through the Music Achievement Council website or your local school music dealer.

Recruitment is a yearlong job. Although many directors don't view recruitment as part of their job, your success in the recruitment process is directly related to your success as an educator. Increased numbers of students will result in the opportunity for you to build a better instrumental music program.

There are many timetables to help you complete the this list. The following is a good place to start. Be sure to remain considerate of your school's master calendar as you address your own needs and the needs of the program. The task is to disseminate information to people in a way that it will be remembered.

One-Year Recruiting Calendar

- In the early fall, or at the end of the previous school year, set up your annual schedule. Include a recruiting meeting with students either after school or, more preferably, in their classrooms where you can be introduced as a "surprise guest." (see page 10) Also schedule a parent meeting (see page 11),and a First Performance Demonstration Concert.
- With the support of the general music teacher(s) from the feeder school(s), work with your principal to schedule at least three visits to each during the fall to visit the music classes of those students who will be incoming the following year. It is important for you to become familiar to these future students.
- February–March: In collaboration with the general music teacher(s), plan an eventful, fun recruiting visit with the students. (One idea might for the general music teacher and the beginning instrumental teacher to play a duet for the students. Another might be to choose one of the songs that the students have learned on their recorders and have them play while you accompany them on an instrument that was brought along for the visit.) The idea is for students to see how much fun it is to be a music-maker!
- April–May: Hold instrument demonstrations and try-outs with students. (Many directors choose to hold the recruiting meeting when students return to school in the fall rather than before school is dismissed the previous year.) Take current students to feeder schools during lunch periods to set up an Instrument Zoo. The same can be done at local malls over the week-ends. Send letters to the parents of all of the incoming students describing the beginning instrumental music program and invite them to a parent meeting (see page 13)? Don't forget to place advance information in the school's newsletter that is generally distributed quarterly. Every parent gets a copy and it's free advertising about your great program.
- One (1) week later: Hold a parent meeting and instrument rental night. Include expectations, lesson schedules and practice commitment. Give parents some tips on how they can guide the practicing at home, even if they do not play. It's important that the students remain motivated and the parents will play a huge role.
- One (1) week after that: Follow up on students who did not enroll.
- Program begins. (If the cycle begins at the end of the prior school year, the program begins when school starts.)
- + 6 to 8 weeks: *First Performance Demonstration Concert* should take place. Involve an administrator—preferably the principal serving as narrator—and make an extra effort to have all parents attend.
- Feb–May: A Mass Band/Parade of Bands/Orchestras/Guitars/Mariachi Ensembles Concert should be held with the recorder classes, the elementary, middle and high school ensembles performing independently and together. Note: Starting concert season earlier in the calendar year gives students a culminating experience before they register for the following year's classes thus potentially avoiding drop-outs.

Recruitment Meeting with Student Checklist

Use this as a checklist of points to be covered using your own personal style. Your music dealer can be of great assistance in this process.

Opening

- Introduce yourself and establish rapport
- Describe the reasons for joining. Highlight the fun, but explain there is work involved in learning an instrument, but that it is rewarding and not so difficult as they might think
- If possible, involve your top current students and be sure they understand that their job is to serve as role model representatives of the program. Young students always want to emulate their older peers.
- Get students actively involved: Clap call and response rhythms, questions about instruments and involve current students in this as well

Demonstration

- Show each instrument — ask its name and family
- Play recruitment DVD or ask current students to perform on the various instruments
- Explain how sound is produced and how pitches are changed and have current students demonstrate
- Demonstrate each instrument, and avoid reinforcing stereotypes (girls play flute, etc.) by choosing appropriate students to demonstrate this.

Instrument Try Out

- Discuss the need for balanced instrumentation
- Have students try instruments and indicate first and second instrument choice
- For a more positive response, never ask, "Who wants to be in the band?" but instead ask, "Who wants to try an instrument?"

Survey

- Explain the survey in simple terms
- Give the survey

Closing

- Collect surveys, and correct them
- Distribute materials for students to take home to parents — you may wish to mail and e-mail this information as well
- Thank students for their time, attention, interest and good behavior
- Develop a recruiting priority list coordinating student assessments, interest and instrument preference
- Thank classroom teachers for their valuable time and help in the recruiting process
- Contact parents and students who have been recommended by other teachers but who have not shown interest; continue your recruiting campaign
- Be sure that the students understand that everyone is welcomed and encouraged to be an integral part your program. It may be a good idea to allow several of your current students to speak about how much the program means to them personally to help eliminate any fears students may have about whether or not they will be successful.

Knowledge is Power

Once students have elected to participate, ensure that both students and parents know all about the music program and the many benefits of being involved. Your first communication should include:

- When new classes are being formed
- The rewards of participating in music
- The idea that active parental support is necessary
- Program details — rehearsal times
- Your expectations and grading policy

Your second communication should include:

- Time and place of parent meetings. All meetings should be as short as possible— let parents know you respect their time
- RSVP form to be signed and returned (see page 13)
- Details about choosing an appropriate instrument
- Information on rental programs or school-owned instruments, if applicable

The Initial Parent Meeting

It is very helpful to have more than one person representing the music program at this meeting. Other members of your staff, your local music dealer representatives, current student and parent representatives, and even your principal are the best participants. Even though this is an extremely important event, under-stand that parents and guardians have very busy schedules, so keep this and other meetings as short as possible. This will allow for maximum attendance.

Parent Meeting Checklist

- Register parents as they arrive—you might prepare a list so that they may simply check off their names
- Consider having current students ready to perform as parents are entering.
- Provide introductory remarks
- Have a music-booster parent make a short, positive statement about the music program and its influence on children.
- Thank parents for their interest in their child's education.
- Explain the beginning music program and the valuable role of the parents.
- Introduce the people represented, including those from the local music dealer.
- Describe physical aptitudes and potential limitations of instrument choices.
- Have the music dealer representative explain instrument options and rental plans available.
- Ease concerns about being stuck with a costly instrument and long hours of practice
- Have your dealers provide brochures about the value of an education in music.
- If you meet with parents individually, have parents look at instruments and advocacy material
- Go over student test scores, teacher evaluations, instrument preferences and recommendations

All of the above are ideas that must be adjusted to your own situation. In some cases, directors like to do the recruiting and meeting with parents on their own. No matter how the director chooses to handle these meetings, it is vital to announce the date of the *First Performance Demonstration Concert*. Emphasize that it is a fun demonstration of the student's progress.

Follow Through

Be aware of critical times in the recruitment process.

Within one week after the instrument demonstration to the students:

- Follow up with all students who have not yet enrolled via a personal telephone call to the parents
- Follow up with all parents reminding them of the meeting date using e-mails and phone calls—enlist the help of your booster organization to assist with personal phone calling, a much more personal means of contact
- Reinforce the benefits of music for their child

Immediately after the parent meeting:

- Immediately after the parent meeting:
- Have a plan to meet with parents who had a schedule conflict with the meeting time
- Make it simple and convenient for parents to visit with you about their child's participation
- Ask your music dealer how he can help with follow-up—parents should see that the dealer is part of the team

Keys to Student Success

It is the director's responsibility to capture the students' attention, sustain their interest and earn their support.

- Realize time conflicts with sports, other classes, school activities and jobs
- Understand each student as an individual
- Build appreciation for the ensemble
- Give recognition for student efforts and accomplishments —badges, medals, printed certificates, tickets to attend special events
- Know that everyone has a fear of failure — constantly praise and reinforce that there is no failure in music. Give formal awards, informal praise and constant encouragement

Be a Music Educator

Ensure that students and parents appreciate the full value of an education in music. In addition to the fulfillment that comes with music-making, students also acquire the 21st Century Skills that will serve them well as they move into adulthood. These include:

- Social skills
- Self-confidence
- Teamwork
- Responsibility
- Coordination

In addition to the above, students will also develop social skills, their sense of responsibility, a level of self-confidence as well as dexterity and coordination. Although highly regarded by students and parents, these benefits are really by-products of music participation. We must never lose sight of the fact that we are also developing students who will have a lifelong appreciation of music. Keep the musical values on the top of your priority list!

Sample Parent Letter: Beginning of Recruitment Process

The following paragraphs may be useful in developing a letter that might work for your situation when contacting parents about your beginning music program.

Each year at this time, students eagerly wait their turn to join our music program. The study of music could be one of the most valuable components in your child's education. Current research shows that playing an instrument increases brain development and—along with developing responsibility, mental discipline, teamwork and self-esteem—will provide enjoyment and fulfillment while fostering a lifelong appreciation of music.

As part of the initial process of identifying interested students, we give a musical aptitude survey to all of the students in your child's grade. We are pleased to report that your child's results were very favorable and that your child is considered a good candidate for the school's instrumental music program.

Our beginning instrumental music class for next year is now being organized. A registration meeting has been scheduled for [day and date] at [time] at [place]. It is important that you attend this meeting as I will review the schedules, provide information about lessons and describe the various instruments as well as answer any questions you may have. We understand you have a busy schedule so the meeting will be short, but informative.

All instruction is free and all that is necessary is for you to obtain an instrument for your child. A quality instrument is the most essential piece of equipment needed for your child's success. Although you may certainly consider the purchase of an instrument for your child at some point, I have asked a representative from _____, our music dealer, to attend our registration meeting to review the reasonable rental plan they have available.

Music is a precious element of daily living. I know that you agree that every child should have the opportunity to participate in music-making, to develop an appreciation for it, and to tap into their hidden talents through the study of it. You can learn more about our program by visiting our website at _____.

I look forward to seeing you at the meeting. If you have any questions, feel free to call me at [phone number] or e-mail me at [e-mail address].

Please complete and return the questionnaire before [date]:

I would like my child to enroll in beginning band _____ orchestra _____ guitar _____ mariachi _____

I will attend the parent meeting Yes _____ No _____

I have a schedule conflict; please call me at _____ or _____

Name of Parent/Guardian _____

Street Address _____ City _____ Zip _____

Home phone_____ Cell phone_____ Email _____

Name of Student _____ Student phone _____

Do you have an instrument? Yes__ No__ If yes, what instrument?_____

Is there a specific instrument that your child is most interested in playing? _____

Please specify your preferred method of contact: Home Phone ___ Cell phone___ Email___ Letter___

Sample Parent Letter: Outlining Goals of the Instrumental Music Program

Our overall goal is to provide positive growth for all students through the study of music. We provide a music study program, which will teach all students to:

- Enjoy working with others
- Expand their knowledge about music and music-making through familiarity with specific compositions
- Experience the thrill of playing an instrument on their own as well as along with, and for, others
- Develop their music literacy skills by cultivating the actual processes involved in music-making and as specified in the Core Music Standards.

Students will also develop their abilities to:

- Focus on the job at hand
- Play an instrument in class
- Prepare for lessons at home
- Listen to the playing of others
- Distinguish individual and ensemble playing skills through critical ear-training
- Play and perform with rhythmic accuracy and melodic feeling
- Play individually and in group settings at school, home and in the community
- Accept constructive criticism from teachers, parents, classmates and the public
- Discover personal fulfillment through a variety of music-making activities

How Parents Can Help

At home:

- Show interest in what your child is learning
- Provide a quality instrument
- Give praise and encouragement
- Arrange a regular time for practice — 15 to 30 minutes a day is better than longer amounts of time every few days
- Find a quiet place for your child to practice without interruptions
- Provide an adjustable-height music stand
- Help and support practice by listening to your child's practice sessions intermittently during the week and providing positive encouragement
- Never make fun of strange sounds made in the beginning
- Help keep a daily record of practice time
- Provide a safe place to keep the instrument
- Keep the instrument in good repair
- Teach your child be on time for lessons and rehearsals
- Encourage your child to play for others
- Have your child video practice sessions then email them to family members— be sure to encourage them to provide positive feedback to your child

At school:

- Keep a record of your child's various music activities and reward them as they progress throughout the year
- Attend all concerts and parent meetings

- Notify the director if your child is going to be absent
- Make sure your child takes his/her instrument and other related music materials to school on lesson and/or rehearsal days
- Teach punctuality
- Be sure your child keeps up with all other classroom studies and assignments
- Visit rehearsals and lessons occasionally
- As needed, discuss the unique needs of your child with the director
- Help with parent activities
- Advocate for music education in the schools

Director's Recruiting Checklist

Planning:
- Recruitment time (spring or fall)
- Meet with the classroom and general music teachers to schedule recruitment visitations and activities
- Select method book(s) and advise your purchasing department or your school music dealer so that they can be made available in a timely manner
- Meet with the school music dealer to reconfirm that he/she will attend the meeting and bring brochures and additional materials as needed
- Meet with the principal and other school personnel to schedule appropriate recruitment events and provide suggestions for how they may assist—if at all possible, involve the principal in this first meeting
- Schedule and publish the dates for all student and parent meetings well in advance
- Determine which instruments will be needed for a balanced instrumentation
- Schedule and publish the dates for the First Performance Demonstration Concert and Mass Band/Orchestra/Guitar/Mariachi concerts

Confirmation:
- Contact principal(s) 3 to 5 days before each scheduled program to reconfirm all particulars
- Have all the necessary supplies needed for each type of meeting ready to go and conveniently at-hand

Student recruitment meeting:
- Arrive 30-60 minutes early
- Meet with principal to review his portion of the meeting
- Have materials well-organized and instruments attractively displayed—your school music dealer may be able to arrange this for you
- Distribute survey cards and pencils
- Introduce your school music dealer(s)
- Distribute parent letters and review
- Collect survey cards
- Distribute posters to teachers for classroom display—provide extras to display in the cafeteria and hallways
- Thank principal, teachers and students

Parent follow-up after the student recruitment meeting:

- Sort survey cards by interest and aptitude
- Select current student and parent leaders to assist in telephone and/or e-mail campaign with parents of the prospective students
- Check for a quality facility to use for the parent meeting and consider involving the high school directors or even ask to have this meeting held in one of the high school facilities—space, ventilation, chairs and tables, locking and unlocking building, and easy-to- follow directions are important to have confirmed and/or available
- Reconfirm meeting time, date and location at least one week in advance
- Conduct phone and e-mail campaign beginning at least one week in advance
- Visit classrooms to remind students of parent meeting

Parent meeting:

- Arrive 30-60 minutes early
- Have parent boosters at the door to welcome prospective parents and students
- Have student performances in the background as all are arriving—perhaps the high school directors could assist with providing students to perform
- Prepare an attractive meeting agenda to provide to attendees
- Meet with parents and students
- Introduce the music dealer representative to meet with the parents and students
- Provide refreshments and have the current student leaders serve the prospective parents

Sample Forms
Sample Student Evaluation by Classroom Teacher

It is recommended that you consider using Google Forms to create a more streamlined method for responses.

Student Name _____ Grade _____

1. Scholastic level:
- A. Outstanding ☐
- B. Good ☐
- C. Average ☐
- D. Poor ☐

2. Scholastic Capabilities:
- A. Outstanding ☐
- B. Good ☐
- C. Average ☐
- D. Poor ☐

3. Work Habits:
- A. Outstanding ☐
- B. Good ☐
- C. Average ☐
- D. Poor ☐

4. Self-Discipline:
- A. Outstanding ☐
- B. Good ☐
- C. Average ☐
- D. Poor ☐

5. Cooperation with Teacher:
- A. Outstanding ☐
- B. Good ☐
- C. Average ☐
- D. Poor ☐

6. Cooperation with Others:
- A. Outstanding ☐
- B. Good ☐
- C. Average ☐
- D. Poor ☐

7. Motivation:
- A. Outstanding ☐
- B. Good ☐
- C. Average ☐
- D. Poor ☐

8. Recommendations:
- A. Student would be a credit to band/orchestra ☐
- B. Band/orchestra could improve this student ☐
- C. Participation questionable ☐
- D. Comments _____
  _____
  _____
  _____

For Directors Only:

Test Score

_____
_____

Recommended Instrument

_____
_____

Sample Telephone Recruiting Script

Hello, my name is _____. I am calling for _____, the band/orchestra/guitar/ mariachi director at _____ [school.] In the recently conducted survey of the _____ grade students at _____ school, _____ [their child's name] had a very high music aptitude rating and showed a lot of interest in learning to play an instrument. We hope you will encourage _____ [their child's name] by giving him/her the opportunity to join our fine instrumental music program.

Sample Instrumental Music Recruiting Meeting Survey
(To be filled out by the parent)

Student's Name _____Parent's Name_____

Street Address _____City_____

Phone _____School _____ Grade _____

What instrument is your child interested in learning? _____

Do you have that instrument? Yes__ No__ Comments_____

_____

_____

Sample Instrumental Music Progress Report

Dear Parent,

This letter is to inform you of your child's progress in our music program. The students have been given weekly assignments to study and practice. The evaluation of all students is based on these assignments plus the level of achievement they demonstrate during class.

Factors considered include the comprehension of the music being studied as demonstrated by your child's performance in rehearsal, attentiveness in class, and assorted homework assignments which include studying and practicing at home.

I am happy to say that _____ [student's name] is doing very well. The following are my suggestions for continued improvement:_____ _____

_____ _____Please call (phone number)_____or e-mail (e-mail address)_____ if you have any questions or concerns.

Sample Report to Parent

(Be sure that this is printed on letterhead if given to the student to take home to the parent. You might also consider emailing it directly to the parent, however please ask parents ahead of time what their preferred method of contact will be – phone, email, letter, etc.)

Date _____ School _____ Call _____

First, let me thank you for helping me to help your child. I thought it might be helpful for me to provide you with an update regarding _____ [student's name] progress in band/orchestra/guitar/mariachi.

After you have read through the information below, please sign and return this letter. Feel free to call me at _____ [phone number] if you have any questions regarding your child's progress.

1. Class preparedness is: Excellent ☐ Good ☐ Fair ☐

2. Completion of required work is: Excellent ☐ Good ☐ Fair ☐

3. Progress is: Excellent ☐ Good ☐ Fair ☐

4. Attitude in class is: _____

_____ (Ex. Cheerful and cooperative, in need of improvement)

5. Was absent on the following days: _____

6. Was tardy on the following days: _____

7. Attended class without: Instrument _____ Music _____

8. Assignment not prepared on: _____ Today's assignment is: _____

_____

_____

9. Needs the following materials: _____

10. Instrument needs the following repair: _____

Comments: _____

_____

Parent/Guardian Signature _____ Date _____

Sample Request for Parents to Participate
in the Parent Support Group/Booster Organization
(Reminder to disseminate via Google Forms, when possible)

Name: _____

Home Phone: _____

 Address: _____ ZIP Code: _____

Place of Employment: _____Work Phone: _____

Work E-mail _____ (used only in case of emergency)

Spouse's Name: _____

Place of Employment: _____Work Phone: _____

Work E-mail _____ (used only in case of emergency)

Preferred method of contact_____

Student's Name: _____School: _____

I/We would like to assist the music program in the following ways
(please check all appropriate areas):

☐ Telephone Committee

☐ Publicity Committee

☐ Programs (printing, designing, etc.)

☐ Ushering at concerts

☐ Assisting teacher during the day — administration and/or office work

☐ Transportation for special concerts, rehearsals or performances during the

    ☐ daytime or ☐ at night or ☐ weekends

☐ Chaperoning student activities

☐ Planning student activities (parties, trips, etc.)

☐ Providing baked goods (student refreshments, receptions, etc.)

☐ Aid in setting up for concerts

☐ As needed

Other (please comment):_____

PART 2 – RETENTION

After successfully recruiting students
for participation in the program,
it is time to focus on retaining them.

The first section of this guide focused on recruitment. In many instances, a variety of challenges from budget constraints to scheduling, can present themselves which can make it more difficult to retain the students. For all practical purposes however, the problems facing the music department, like politics, are local. While national leaders tackle national problems, you must tackle the problems of your own music department in your own community. Whatever they are and whatever their urgency, chances are they are not unique to you. This section of the Recruitment and Retention Guide is designed to help you increase the rate of retention in your program.

Public Knowledge Is Public Support

Every music educator must be able to explain, demonstrate and promote the value of music and define its role in the curriculum. Besides being able to articulate the benefits of an education in music, educators must actively pursue opportunities to advocate for music education in their communities. It is important to remember that many people confuse the music program's utility with its academic value. They understand the goals and achievements of teaching performance skills, promoting school spirit and public relations, encouraging group discipline and teaching cooperation. Although you should include these points and those cited in the most current research, you must always reinforce the goal of music education for its intrinsic value. You should concentrate on musicianship, aesthetic awareness and the study of high-quality literature as well as providing entertainment. Often, the public will join the decision makers in eliminating music programs due to pressure to reduce budgets or to increase the teaching of the so-called basics. You will draw the public to your side however, if you believe and demonstrate that music is more than a tool for teaching other subjects, but rather an essential part of a well-rounded education that will provide students with fulfilling and enriching experiences.

Preserve Your Most Valuable Resource — Your Students

- Make the aesthetic pleasure one derives from music the most compelling reason to participate
- Foster pride and group recognition
- Give credit to individual accomplishments
- Don't include fear in your teaching approach
- Show interest in the music they like (even if you don't like it)
- Make sure all instruments are in excellent playing condition
- Remind parents that repair services are included in most rental contracts
- Make instrument care an important part of the beginner class
- Provide aids — charts, booklets, etc., many of which are provided by manufacturers and publishers
- Seek help when you have a problem — talk to other directors, music dealers, manufacturer and publisher representatives, and attend conventions and clinics

Ideas for Retaining Students and Recruiting Parents

- Use testimonials from students, especially in reaching other students
- Get your message out as far and wide as possible
- Get parents involved in your program
- Show parents how they can help their child during home practice
- Remind parents that every beginner, even Moza rt, needed to practice
- Put on a *First Performance Demonstration Concert*
- Continually keep in touch with parents send brief, well-timed e-mails highlighting group successes and proven social and academic benefits
- Post your successes on social media and do it often
- Use photos of students to promote your program as often as permissible by your school

Marketing the Instrumental Music Program

Traits and characteristics of the SUCCESSFUL teacher:

- Organizes and prepares all facets of the program with efficiency
- Employs an open, nonthreatening manner with all students
- Maintains a professional appearance
- Uses an energetic and vivacious approach to teaching
- Possesses a good sense of humor
- Understands students' likes and attitudes (is hip and with it)
- Participates actively in professional development activities
- Admits mistakes and learns from them
- Supports all students
- Cooperates with other school staff and administrators
- Considers new ideas
- Puts in the time that it takes to get the job done
- Remains aware of students' time and schedules
- Knows the craft and how to relate to the students
- Moves through the class often
- Maintains a high degree of self-discipline and effective classroom management
- Gives praise and support
- Always working to improve the musical experience for the students
- Serves as an exemplary role model—what they see is what you get

Internal:

- Organizes class time with a variety of activities
- Maintains high standards
- Keeps students on task by keeping talking to a minimum
- Cultivates a high degree of interest in all students
- Uses a pro-active approach to recruiting throughout the entire school year
- Schedules short concerts (at all levels)
- Communicates clear goals for individuals and groups

External:

- Maintains a positive relationship with administration, fellow teachers and support staff
- Communicates regularly with parents and guardians
- Performs often in the school and the community
- Maintains a professional look and demeanor with all performing groups
- Closely scripts all comments at performances
- Performs music within the technical ability of the performers
- Develops connections among school, parents and community
- Advocates for music education

Reasons Students Leave the Program

Personal:
- Failure in academic classes
- Poor practice habits
- Wrong choice of instrument
- Laziness
- Involved in too many other activities
- Problems in transporting larger instruments

Home:
- Family moves away
- Broken or unplayable instrument
- Problems in transporting larger instruments
- Poor home environment
- Lack of suitable practice area
- Lack of parental support

School:
- Not enough class meetings to sustain progress
- Frequent interruptions in class schedule
- Difficulty in academic subjects
- Disciplinary problems
- Lack of administrative support

Teacher:
- Inappropriate instructional methods and materials
- Teacher moves too rapidly
- Teacher does not make goals clear
- Teacher talks too much
- Classes are too large
- Teacher is not enthusiastic
- Teacher is too negative and sarcastic

Actions that Help Retain Students
- Develop personal and group pride
- Schedule a First Performance Demonstration Concert as soon as possible at the beginning of each school year
- Improve communication with parents
- Evaluate yourself continually
- Strive to understand each student as an individual
- Check student instruments regularly
- Hone your recruitment techniques
- Teach instrument care and maintenance and feel free to ask your school music dealer for assistance in this process
- Maintain an open line of communication with the administrative team
- Being positive and enthusiastic
- Smile!
- Plan for and provide a great lesson each and every day. Your students deserve your very best in the same way that you deserve their's